the
rhymes
in
my
mind

Also by this author

My Heart on Your Sleeve

The Odd Collection

the rhymes in my mind

Samantha Turner

Copyright © 2020 Samantha Turner

All rights reserved, including the right to reproduce this book, or portions thereof in any form. No part of this text may be reproduced, transmitted, downloaded, decompiled, reverse engineered, or stored, in any form or introduced into any information storage and retrieval system, in any form or by any means, whether electronic or mechanical without the express written permission of the author.

The views expressed in this work are solely those of the author and do not necessarily reflect the views of the publisher, and the publisher hereby disclaims any responsibility for them.

Cover design by Richard Pilkington

ISBN: 978-1-915889-02-7

PublishNation
www.publishnation.co.uk

Contents

Introduction

Forget You Not

Heaven

Mother

Your Mountain

Mystery Moon

Sweet Music

No Money and Nothing to Do

Peace

Faith

Play Pretend

Not So Grim Up North

The Air of Change

Autumn

Winter Solstice

My Mask

The Constant Battle

No Age

Coming Back

Me

Desire for The Dark

Time

Darren's Poem

Afterword

Welcome to my new collection
of random poetry.

I write because I am compelled to.

I may be brushing my teeth
or walking in the rain
when the words begin to form
in my mind.

There is no method
or planning in my writing,
maybe that is why the poems
seem to jump
from one subject
to another.

Forget You Not

I know you are afraid my friend
The world is suddenly strange
There is a real threat of danger
And life out there has changed

Do you have everything you need my friend?
Can I help in any way?
Not just with doorstep drop-offs
Or words through windowpane

For sustenance is more than
Merely bread and tea
What about the laughter
Our chats and memories?

When all of this is over
And survivors come outdoors
To celebrate with family
Not take for granted anymore

The liberty and open space
The birdsong and the sky
Maybe will mean much more to us
The joy we cannot buy

The streets will all be bustling
The parks all filled with play
This world will seem much brighter
Through eyes which once were grey

With gratitude and huge relief
That danger is averted
Life will pour upon the world
No city still deserted

But what becomes of you my friend?
Still trapped inside your home
The isolation rules are over
But for you it is the norm

For you are old and shaky
Alone since Mary passed
Just a photo on the mantelpiece
You smile and she smiles back

My friend will they remember you
Still watching through the glass?
Will greed and self-return?
Will kindness walk on past?

I don't want you to worry friend
For lessons have been learned
You will no longer be forgotten
Or left alone and scared

Can you hear me now my friend?
I'm knocking on your door
There's a party in the street outside
Let me help you with your coat

Heaven

Come; sit with me on a lazy afternoon
We shall picnic in the meadow
Where the wildflowers bloom

In such perfect idleness
Memories may stir
Like ripples on the water
Watch them fade without a care

Bare feet and laughter
Cloudless blue skies
Warm breeze on freckled skin
The soft tickle of butterflies

Time means nothing here
We are young forever more
For life began and ended
While we found our way back home

Mother

As little girls we sat on your knee
Had cuddles and told you our woes
Played 'round and round the garden'
And 'This little piggy' with our toes

All through our teens
And stupid mistakes
You always stood by us
No matter the shame

I want you to know
We have always felt loved
Always felt blessed
That you are our Mum

Now you are older
The children you raised
Will never forsake you
Or the memories made

Your Mountain

Take your breath
Take your time
Take in the view
One foot in front of the other
The summit will wait for you

There is no rush or judgement
Let others pass on by
You are not here for them
Let the mountain be your guide

In fellowship or solitude
We all walk for a reason
United by our love of the fells
Their beauty and our freedom

Mystery Moon

I rise early to see the moon
Before it sets behind the black
Skeleton branches of our tree
The yellow white orb with an eerie glow
Somehow makes me feel both ageless
And ancient at the same time
I am captivated
This lunar spectacle draws me in
Like a magpie to a diamond
Shining and enticing in its wonder
The moon shines on us all
The early morning workers
Relishing their coffee with bleary eyes
Remnants of a dream still cloudy in their mind
On the tiny mice that scurry in the grass
Illuminating their secrets to the night owl that
hunts them
But this moon, this special, bright, glorious full
moon is shining for me
Just me
I am alone and the moon sees me
For one magical moment, I know
I know everything
Then it is gone

Sweet Music

I am hypnotised by your melody
You play my heartstrings like a harp
A rhythm that is haunting me
The distant drumming in the dark
Like the piper in the woods
You lure me in, a trance-like state
I am attracted to your heartbeat
And the music that it makes

No Money and Nothing to Do

I didn't get dressed today
There really was no point
No-one came to visit
And I wasn't going out

I didn't clean my teeth today, I forgot
I haven't eaten anyway
So maybe it doesn't matter
If I brush them or not

I will shower in the morning
Maybe wash my hair
Put on a bit of makeup
But there's no-one here to care

Daytime TV is awful
All funeral ads and loans
Cancel the licence
I have no interest anymore

Social media
What are all the happy people doing today?
Such fantastic lives they lead
Exotic holidays

Sightseeing and spending
Designer clothes
I'm turning them off
It's too depressing to know

Anyway, I'm tired
I might go back to bed
No money and nothing to do
I may as well be dead

Peace

Time does not matter
No clock is ticking for me
I can stay here in lazy contentment
Nowhere I need to be

Blue sky above
Grass between my toes
Listening to the river
It's ever trickling flow

On and on
Continuous to the sea
Oh, how happy I am
To finally be free

Faith

Who is it that I talk to in my head?
Is it you that I pray to as I lay in my bed?
I do not know if I believe in religion
But I do know I believe in you

I asked you for a sign once
To show me the way to go
But when the sign was given
I was too afraid to know

I tell you my worries
Give thanks for your help
I pray you give me courage
Long life and good health

I have never fully read a bible
I do not know the Lord's Prayer
Yet I feel you all around me
I believe that you are there

Small steps, a toe in the water
I am making my way to you

Play Pretend

The birds are calling for me, Robin, Blackbird
and Wren
Fill the feeders, change the water
For a minute let's play pretend

Thrown over the back of the sofa
Your t-shirt is where you left it
Socks still stuffed inside your worn trainers
I told you off for being messy

I can lie star-shaped in the bed now
Your leg hair no longer makes me itch
The quilt is all mine
But it smothers me with loneliness
I miss you all the time

The birds are calling for me, Robin, Blackbird
and Wren
I need to fill the feeders, change the water
Play pretend

Not So Grim Up North

Some may say it's grim up north
All chimneys, smoke, and fog
The men all wearing flat caps
With walking sticks and clogs

But on these streets of cobbled stones
And alleys back to back
In terraced houses row by row
No sunshine does it lack

Mam is keeping busy
It's wash day for the women
With dolly tub and rubbing board
And clothes pegs in her piny

Dad's gone working down the pit
Hewing coal with all the men
Our Nancy's at the cotton mill
And I'm off school again

When weather's good and Dad's been paid
We pack a bag and catch the train

Blackpool tower, beach and sea
Children's faces bright with glee
Funfair, donkeys, fish, and chips
My favourite are the crispy bits

Sometimes we go to Wigan park
A basket filled with scones
We'll picnic in a shady spot
Relax the whole day long

Friday night my Dad goes pub
A pint well-earned he says
I hear him whistling up the path
As he makes his merry way

My Auntie lives in Cumbria
My Uncle has a farm
There's lots of lakes and mountains there
So beautiful and calm

I'd like to take a boat upon
A lake like that someday
Sail to a little island
From school I'd hide away

Our street at home is not like that
But we do have fields and cows
Mam sends me to the shop sometimes
For milk from Mr Brown

There is a big house on the hill
A mighty hall called Haigh
With servants for the rich folk
And a keeper on the gate

I dream that I'm a lady
All posh in dresses made
From satin pink and lavender
Hemmed with pretty lace

I'd walk among the gardens
Just to take the air
Saunter among the flowers
I wouldn't have a care

The only way that I'll see Haigh
Is working with the cook
Or cleaning out the fires
All head to toe in soot

Maybe I'll meet a handsome groom
We'll marry in the spring
A ribbon on my finger
While he can't afford a ring

Or I could be an entertainer
The North has bred a few
Mam tells me I'm a dreamer
To be quiet now, eat my stew

We've George Formby, cleaning windows
Ukulele songs that linger
Stan Laurel makes us laugh
On stage and screen acting daft

Beatrix Potter, Peter Rabbit
Fame and talent
Up north we have it

All said and done though
Life's not bad
I have a loving Mam and Dad

I never go hungry
No holes in my socks
Dreaming's alright but
I'm happy with my lot

Doors are always open
And neighbours are our friends
In times of fear and trouble
All help to make amends

Laughter from the children
Playing in the street
Gossip from the women
With everyone they meet

We fierce and loyal Northern folk
Are proud and stubborn too
But even though we don't have much
We'd gladly share with you

So, come and pay a visit
There's pie fresh from the oven
I'll lay an extra place for you
Let Mam know that you're coming

The Air of Change

Summers end and we fall into autumn as the
colours begin to turn.
Spectacles of bronze as the trees preserve their
life.
Decaying leaves give childish joy as we crunch
our way across the covered
earth and nature's jewels adorn the trees with
shiny delights.
A rush of animals gather up their precious
bounty in haste, for soon the land
will be bare, the ground solid with frost.
Skeleton branches create a haunting stillness
as hibernation takes hold.
The whisper of winter, the hush of cold, until
the air changes and the
promise of spring once more

Autumn

Death of leaves, early dark
But death of one means life
The illusion of fire brings not heat
But whispers of cold in canopies of amber and gold

This is the season that I await
Such joy does it create, in me

I do not fear the winter snow
Or the silence of the dark
Nor twisted branches of the trees
That are sleeping still and stark

Curious, my eyes are ever to the sky
Searching without blindness or strain
The stars they are eternal
Only hidden as the sun does rise again

Here I shall wait
For the burning light to fade
Hiding in the shadows
Of the cool and silent shade

While others may mourn
The dying of the light
We awake in celebration
The velvet dark and I

Winter Solstice

On this winter solstice
When longest night
Brings hope to all
Who long for light

Life that is sleeping
Will slowly rouse
As snowdrops peep
From ancient ground

The promise of warmth
And sunlit skies
Buds on the trees
The birth of new life

Winter's dark gave peace and rest
Preserving energies for spring
Love and joy for you and yours
The coming year will bring

My Mask

Skulls are hideous and frightening
Reminding us of what monsters we are
underneath
This mask of skin that hides the truth
Can be shaped into any disguise
But peel back the flesh
And there is the proof
Concealed beneath
Blood vessels and lies

The Constant Battle

Fluffy pyjamas, cosy slippers
Coffee, biscuits, and massive knickers
I sit and wonder, ' will I ever be thin?'
As my hand reaches back into the biscuit tin

Skinny jeans and platform shoes
No bingo wings or heavy boobs
I can see it now, Me size twelve
By Christmas I'll be a skinny elf

No covering up my bulky size
Trying to avoid judgmental eyes
Or hiding wrappers in the bin
Wondering why I can't get thin

I can't deny, I like to eat
And chocolate is my friend
So are chips and crisp and gin
I know I can't pretend

That salad is a joy to eat
Or exercise a pleasure
Boobs a flying, two black eyes
And thighs rubbing together

No thanks, I'll pass it's not for me
I'll start tomorrow. Or not, maybe…

No Age

We are no longer young. We are ageing and a little grey.
Our bones crack and our bodies ache.
So what?
Let us paddle in the sea anyway.
Let us have a go on the swings.
Let's get tipsy on gin and dance in the garden like we used to.
Let's kiss like teenagers and feel skin against skin.
We are still here. We are alive.
And I for one think that is wonderful!

Coming Back

I am coming back to you
When all of this is done
Even if the light has faded
And leaves are golden brown

If summertime means solitude
Alone in gardens bare
My warmth will come from sunshine
My conversation from the birds

Do not focus on the sadness
Or things we may have missed
The earth is merely resting
Taking time to deal with this

I am coming back to you
We all just need to wait
To heed the constant warning
Stay home. Stay safe.

Me

My stomach isn't flat
And my thighs meet in the middle
My bottom is on the large side
Boobs wobble when I giggle

I'm not exactly fat
But I'm definitely not thin
Mother Nature gave me scars
To remind me where I've been

My hair's not poker straight
But neither is it curly
The process got confused
As I was born a little early

I've a gap between my teeth
And a very small top lip
My waist is only narrow
Compared to my wide hips

I've freckles in the summer
In winter, deathly pale
Laughter lines and ageing
Begin to show upon my face

Green-brown eyes
Depending on the light
A slightly pointed chin
My cheekbones are high

I would describe myself as average
Neither a beauty nor a hag
Just somewhere in between
And I'm alright with that

Desire for The Dark

Shine your light upon me
Bring me out from the shadows and the grey
Illuminate my lies and mistakes
But love me anyway
Inside and out
Kiss my scars
Heal and make me whole
Always find me
When I lose myself
You know my soul
Is inclined to roam
Searching for that other place
Where the fireflies dance
And all fear is erased
So, keep your light shining
As a beacon
Burning brighter than my desire
To go

Time

The hum of a kettle boiling.
Middle-aged fingers dip into the tea-bag pot.
The clinking of spoons against cups.
Watching the clock.
Not quite yet, the tea will be too cold.
The familiar sound of a key turning in the lock.
The light comes on as the fridge door opens
Pour in the milk now
He is home, the tea just right.
He smells of machinery and sweat
Calloused hands with bitten nails wrap
gratefully around the steaming cup
A tired smile and closed eyes
As she asked
'How was your shift, love?'
A hint of guilt in her voice

I view these images now as they were
In cinematic slides of a child's mind
And I see myself as her
For it is me who stands by the kettle each night
The fingers around the cup are still calloused
and bitten
Though they belong to a different man in a
another era
A memory repeated, time mimicking time
And life goes on.

The following poem was written
by my husband Darren
on our ten-year wedding
anniversary.
He is not a writer,
but he wrote this for me.

You walked into my life
I knew it would be forever
No regrets, you make my life better

Ten years today our souls entwined
Making our vows until the end of time

Our bodies will fail
But our souls will live on
Deep in the tree roots, someday forgotten
But never gone

Afterword

Write what is in your heart.
Write because
you want people
to read
and enjoy
your words.
I hope that you have enjoyed mine.

www.ingramcontent.com/pod-product-compliance
Lightning Source LLC
Chambersburg PA
CBHW070340120526
44590CB00017B/2968